Afternoon of a Sadhu

Afternoon of a Sadhu

A Memoir of India

Violet Snow

Lucid Press

Copyright © 2012 Ellen J. Carter
All rights reserved.
ISBN-10: 1-46994-999-7
ISBN-13: 978-1-469-94999-4

Manufactured in the
United States of America

Lucid Press
PO Box 63
Phoenicia NY 12464

To Sparrow and Sylvia

and

to my parents,
who put up with so much.

CONTENTS

1	Choice	1
2	Practice	27
3	The Real Thing	53
	Epilogue	95
	Glossary of Hindi Words	99

Afternoon of a Sadhu

1 CHOICE

When I was in India, I gave away my money and most of my possessions and became a beggar for a month and a half. A few Western travelers take this path. India shakes them like dice. Life there smashes Western preconceptions, and once those are gone, anything becomes possible.

It was 1978. I was 22, and I'd been wandering around India and Sri Lanka for almost a year, seeking adventure, enlightenment, and a boyfriend. I was almost ready to give up on all three, weary and in despair. On a bright January morning, I sat down at the Sunshine Café in Colaba, Bombay's hotel district, and ordered tea. The man at the next table turned and asked if I had any antibiotics. He was gaunt and stringy-haired, with skin the ghastly parchment yellow of the opiate addict.

"I have this infection," he explained with a faint English accent, showing me the lump of pus on his forearm. That's where he fixes, I thought. I had encountered junkies in India, but I'd never made friends with one, so this gruesomeness was new and fascinating.

"I don't have any pills," I replied, "but I have some antibiotic cream that might help. I'll get it for you later. I'm staying at the hostel across the street."

"Thanks a lot. I'd really appreciate it. Have you just arrived in Bombay?"

"Yeah, yesterday, from Goa."

"Where are you going next?"

"Oh, I don't know. Nepal maybe. By the way, do you know where I can get some visa pictures taken?"

"Yeah, sure. I'll take you there."

Abruptly, he turned back to the Indian man sitting at his table.

"Did you hear about this business with Richard, it's too much! I get involved to help out, and all I get for it is trouble."

"What happened?" asked the Indian. "I heard some German guy got his passport ripped off. You got it back for him?"

"Yeah, he was running around blabbing about it, and we knew who did it, I mean Richard's a friend, but that's bad business, stealing passports, and he wasn't being cool about it, either. So Gilles and I went to talk it out of him, and everything woulda been okay except the hotel manager went and called the cops. Then Richard, the bastard, what a friend, tries to pin it on me! The cops take my passport, Gilles and I get kicked out of the hotel. For trying to help! But people in Colaba know me, they all tell police I'm okay. I'm always straight with people, everyone told them."

"That's right, Garry," the other man nodded, smoothing down his shiny hair. "You always honest, all Colaba people know that."

"I've done a lot of favors for people here, a lot of business and never cheated anyone, you know that, Misra. And now this son-of-a-bitch Richard tries to drag me down with him. It makes me sick."

"No, you good man, Garry. Everyone in Colaba telling. Don't worry. So what you doing now?"

"Ah, I'm not feeling too good, got this infection, and now I have to go to the police and get my passport back. Been staying at Hassan's place. Don't get much sleep there, but they're good company. Yeah, I'm the night manager." He snickered, looking at me. "Nice guys. Made me the night manager." He laughed again, and I smiled blankly. "Come on," he said, "I'll take you to the photo shop."

We stepped out into the sun and headed down Best Marg. In four blocks we were stopped three times by men who shook Garry's hand and drew him aside to talk. At last we progressed to the photo shop, and I had my picture taken.

"So what's there to do on a Monday afternoon in Bombay?" I asked. "You must know this town pretty well."

"You like to smoke opium?"

"Sure, why not?"

"Let's get a cab." He told the driver to take us to Sukalaji Street.

Sukalaji Street. I grew up in Poughkeepsie, New York; not actually in that upstate city but in a housing development molded around hills and woods outside of town. It was the ultimate in semi-affluent middle-class security. Ever since I left the cozy lap of Overlook Estates, I had been trying to escape the boredom that the place had warned me was my lot. But it isn't easy to fight the habits of suburban banality, and even though I was in exotic India, my adventures had been coming out half-baked. The sex and party mania on the nude beaches of Goa had been as unromantic as Sri Lanka's meditation retreats, and I was feeling like a failure as an adventuress. Now, in the space of less than an hour, I had jumped the tracks of convention in no less than three ways: I had made the acquaintance of a bona fide junkie, I was heading for an opium den, and I was about to visit a mysterious place called Sukalaji Street.

I always rode buses to save money, but when we arrived, I paid the driver. Garry apologized for being broke, and I shrugged. Middle-class rebels have to pay for excitement. I looked around. We were on a narrow lane in a Muslim quarter. The shops were like shops anywhere in India, with wooden shutters open to reveal men seated among their wares: provision shops with rice, lentils, spices, candles, soap; cigarette and betel nut stalls; jewelers with glass cases full of silver and gold ornaments; metalware shops; vendors of plastic buckets and household goods; tailors and cloth merchants; streetcorner hawkers of roasted peanuts and chickpeas, dates, fruit, *chai* (rich, sweet, milky tea), bangles, penknives, religious posters. But there were no post cards, cheap Western clothes, handcarved wood items, brass ewers, or any of the other tourist paraphernalia sold aggressively on the streets of Colaba. And the people were different. Men in round caps stared at me as I swished by in my flowered skirt. A single woman veiled in black scurried past and disappeared. I was self-conscious, but I enjoyed feeling unique, and Garry was here to protect me.

He pointed to the pastel shutters on the two-storied buildings across the street. "Those are brothels."

"Oh." I was thrilled.

We turned down an alley, climbed a creaking staircase, and knocked discreetly at a door. We were admitted to a crowded little room reeking of sweetish smoke. Several Europeans sat along the wall, passing a chillum of hashish mixed with tobacco. Middle-aged Indians lay on their sides around a charcoal lantern, their heads propped up on bricks. Garry motioned for me to lie beside a second lamp and respectfully asked the old attendant for a chip of *chandu*. The man silently prepared the viscous syrup, rolling it from the small brass chip onto a slender rod and then burning it over the lamp. He scraped the *chandu* over a tiny hole in a wooden cylinder, which he held near the coals, nodding at me to pull on the pipe. After two more repetitions of this procedure, I had smoked half the chip. "That's enough. I think more would make me sick. You want the rest?" My only other opium experience had left me retching in a stinking bathroom.

"No, I never smoke opium," Garry answered. "I only eat and fix—O, morph, junk in general. And cocaine. Give the rest to him. *Apke liye, babiji.*" The old man nodded to me graciously. I paid him two and a half rupees: thirty cents. "Let's go over to my place," said Garry. "We can relax there."

We went out to the bright street. "How do you feel?" Garry asked.

"Nice and slow and soft. Not sick at all. In general, though, I prefer uppers. I'm pretty slow to begin with."

"You want to do some coke? An eighth is enough for the two of us. That's only fifty rupees."

"An eighth of what? A gram?"

"Right, a gram."

"Um. Sure, why not?" Fifty rupees was only six dollars.

Street, alley, stairs, and a noisy hallway brought us to the home and office of three Muslim brothers who dealt cocaine. A single shabby room crammed with furniture. In one corner, a concrete stall with dripping tap. A calendar on the wall, with a picture of the Kaaba in Mecca and sweeping Arabic letters. From the paint-speckled bureau, Hassan took a small vial, peering at me uncertainly. He and Akbar silently watched me sniff my hits through a rolled-up rupee note, while

Garry injected his with swift efficiency. I was enthralled. I had never watched anyone fix before.

We progressed from an eighth to a quarter and then another quarter. With each successive hit, Garry's behavior became more bizarre. As soon as he released the belt from his arm, he began to jerk like a marionette, jumping to his feet, bending arms, legs, neck in spasms. His voice too jerked and pulled, words tumbling out and then drawling, fading off to a sharp insuck of air before the next outburst. By now he knew I was not judging him, but he saw that he had become too unnatural for me.

He grinned. "Don't be embarrassed. It's pretty grotesque, isn't it? But I don't care. I feel good, I don't care how I look. So why should you care? I don't care what people think any more. It used to bother me, but I've learned not to worry about it. I'm a junkie. I've been a junkie for ten years. That's what I am, why should I hide it? If people don't like it, that's their problem. I'm a fag,

I like men, why should I lie about it? Everyone's afraid of what other people will think, but for me it's more important to be honest. I don't want to hurt anyone, I just want to get high with my friends and have a good time. And learn a little. That's life, isn't it? Learning?"

"That's what it is to me. Learning. I can't even tell a good life from a bad life. But whatever happens, I can learn something from it."

"Exactly." He sat down and leaned close. "What do you think of all this? What do you really think?"

"I don't think anything. It's all new to me. I'm just watching myself to see how I feel."

"And how do you feel?"

"High." We giggled. "It's exciting because it's new. I'm not scared, you know, of this place, I mean. I couldn't be here without you, though."

"Come on, let's go for a walk."

It was dark out. The drug gave me a clairvoyant wisdom. I was on a high wire, with the world mapped out below, and it was thrilling to look down and see how far I could fall. But there was no fear because I knew my balance was perfect. And I knew that Garry was there on the high wire too, and it made me feel wonderfully close to him. Still, it took me a while to open up to him.

As we walked down Sukalaji Street, women cooed and beckoned from the doorways. We crossed the street for a better look at the painted, pursed lips, the long fingers fluttering obscenely.

"Kind of disgusting, isn't it?" he said. "So many times I've come down this street and thought of buying one, but I never have."

"Why not? It could be interesting, if you were in the mood."

"I guess I've just never been in the mood. Anyway, I prefer men, mostly. You'd better take my arm. It's safer. I don't mean to come on with you, please don't worry about that. I've got a wife, after all. We lived together for a year. She's in Japan now. You know, women say that men who've been with men make better lovers. More sensitive."

"Yeah? Makes sense, I guess."

We walked a couple of blocks and entered a house. Garry shook hands with a fat man wearing a fez. They spoke in Urdu for several minutes before they unclasped hands. Garry and I sat as the man left. Tea was brought. I looked around at the opulent striped curtains and red carpet and wondered where we were.

"So how do you like Sukalaji Street?" he asked.

"I'm fascinated. I don't usually get to see this part of town."

"Yeah, it's off the tourist track. I like it here. Good people. A lot of women don't like Muslims because they get hassled by the men."

"I spent six months in Muslim countries, and I didn't have much trouble. I think it depends on how you act. You can't treat them like Western men."

"That's true. You seem to know how to behave. The boys at Hassan's are quite impressed with you. They don't see many Western women around here."

I was pleased. "People say Islamic culture is repressive, and I wouldn't want to be a Muslim woman, but sometimes I envy them. Everything is prescribed—they know exactly what to do. They don't have to make a million choices about their lives. I have all this freedom, but I don't know what to do with it."

"Yeah, it's very simple for them. You wouldn't like it, though."

"Of course not."

"Maybe you don't know what to do, but you can experiment and figure out what you want."

"But I'm sick of experimenting. I'm not getting anywhere. I can't meditate, can't write, can't find a boyfriend. I'm just going around in circles."

"Except here—you go straight up." He winked, and we laughed.

"But then do you come straight down?" I asked him.

"Sometimes. But you know you can always go back up."

I shook my head. "The drug culture's too heavy for me. I'm here because I'm curious, but I haven't got the nerve to live this way. I can't deal with people like you can."

"It takes certain instincts, but one can develop them. Oh, but I'm not trying to talk you into becoming a junkie."

"I know. God, it's nice to meet someone who talks about real things, not just 'Where have you been in India?' You're the first interesting person I've met in months."

"I try to keep my brain alive," he said. "Some junkies just live for drugs and lose touch with reality. But you're kind of unusual yourself. Not a typical tourist."

"I hope not."

Most of my life I had alternated between suspecting I was a rare and wonderful person and fearing I was a complete loser. Because of my shyness, I seldom met people who told me I was a rare and wonderful person. Hearing this reassurance was a great pleasure. My confidence went upward, my inhibitions—thanks to the cocaine—went downwards, and I became animated, not my usual condition.

Garry and I talked for another hour, covering topics from high school to the writings of R.D. Laing. He told me frightening stories of near-death in hospitals, and I told him about teaching English in Tehran. I was awed by his knowledge of Indian politics. He was sure that Indira Gandhi, although she had been forced to resign only two years earlier, would soon be re-elected. (She was, three years later.) We exchanged a few intimate secrets, and by the time we returned to Hassan's, I was bursting with platonic love.

Back at the coke den, we dug into another quarter. The rising dosage excited me, but the money was worrisome. In came Ali, the only brother who was not an addict. This tall, graceful boy reminded me of one of my meditation teachers, a Buddhist monk. While Garry argued in Urdu with Akbar, Ali said to me gravely, "I was addict to morphine six months. My parents paid for me stay in hospital for cure. Now I never take these drugs, only hashish smoking." As he spoke, I watched his long fingers fold and arabesque, just like the monk's.

Suddenly he leaned forward, lowering his voice. "You listen me. You take plane, go home. This no good place for you."

I panicked. Of course he was right. What was I doing here? Not my natural habitat. I look at Garry, a parchment-faced freak bobbing and jabbing at the air as he enticed me to ruin.

No. I was here of my own free will. I was high on coke, and I knew what I was doing. I looked at Garry again, and he smiled. Ali was being melodramatic.

"Listen, can we afford another quarter?"

I was silent. I was too high already. And I had spent almost forty dollars in a country where I usually lived on two dollars a day. Suddenly I wanted to get out and think. "I have to go, I'm sorry." I saw the craving in his face. "I'll buy you another eighth, all right? I don't want any more."

He came downstairs to hail me a taxi, and we agreed to meet at the Sunshine at noon. He looked worried. "I'm sorry, it's the money," I said. "I have to think."

Back at the hostel, I sat in the dark among wheezing and snoring women. It was late, but the coke in my blood kept me wide awake. My mind moved boldly and clearly through the elements of my dilemma. Money. What was the true monetary value of this night, my first night of real adventure? What was the monetary value of a friendship with a man who talked about life instead of making chitchat? But could I afford this friendship and this lifestyle? If I kept it up, my money would be gone in a week, and then what would I do? I couldn't live like Garry.

At this point I recalled my sadhu fantasy. A few months earlier, I had read the autobiography of Sri Ram Das, a South Indian spiritual master. He had spent many years as a sadhu, a religious person who renounces possessions and wanders India, begging food and shelter from pious Hindus who welcome the opportunity to improve their karma by serving the servants of God.

What had always fascinated me about saints was that they did the opposite of what seemed logical. Christ requested mercy for his killers, not revenge. When the Buddha was threatened by an angry priest, he spoke sweetly to the man and eventually earned his devotion. Ram Das, freezing and starving on a stormy night in the wilds, told his disciple to relax. "We will die if Brahma wills it so. Otherwise we will be saved. There is no cause to worry." A shepherd in search of a strayed lamb found them and took them to his home, saving their lives.

The sadhu's path sounded like a strenuous but radiant way to live, released from the complications and decisions of civilized existence, whittled down to the basics of survival. I had fantasized losing my belongings through some accident and being forced to live on the donations of villagers, evolving ultimately into a carefree wanderer like Ram Das, freed from attachment to earthly goods and possessing a secret joy that would lead some day to enlightenment.

This idle thought came after I read the saint's life. Now, faced with a concrete money problem, I considered: why not give up my possessions deliberately and live out this fantasy? I had heard of other Westerners becoming sadhus. The thin blonde English girl I'd met in Dharamsala was rumored recently to have chucked everything, clothes, passport, portable stereo, in the Ganges and taken saffron robes at Rishikesh. Of course, she was already a little mad when I met her. It was an absurd idea but not unheard of.

The absurdity, in fact, attracted me, especially after meeting Garry. He was living a life that I considered absurdly self-destructive, yet he seemed intensely alive and morally good, with an integrity that I lacked. Like a sadhu, he sacrificed security and put himself at the mercy of others, always living on the edge of danger. Especially when he was broke, he was never sure where he would get his next fix, without which he would be desperately ill. But some friend always provided for him, because his generosity endeared him to the people around him. Somehow he had made his way through ten years of drug addiction without dying, without losing his reason, and without landing an extended jail sentence. I was impressed by the courage, faith, and savvy it took to live that way. If I put myself at the mercy of the universe, maybe I would develop the same qualities. I wanted to live on the edge too. Perhaps the coke was making me overconfident, but I knew I could do it.

The more I sat and thought, the more giddy I felt. Unable to sleep, I made plans. I wasn't sure I was entitled to dress in saffron—after all, I hadn't been initiated by a guru—but if I wore white and shaved my head, I ought to be easily identifiable as a sadhu. I could start out in Benares. Being the holiest of Hindu cities, it was not only the most appropriate starting point, but it was also full of sadhus and therefore undoubtedly full of places for sadhus to eat and sleep. Then when I was ready, I would set out into the countryside and ask the villagers to provide for my needs.

What if no one would feed me? I was willing to fast if the lifestyle required it. I pictured myself wasting away by the roadside in lotus position (well, half-lotus at least) until some passerby took pity and offered me food. Could I really do that? I would find out.

AFTERNOON OF A SADHU

For how long would I be a sadhu? I felt that if I were deeply sincere, I would do it for the rest of my life. But I didn't quite have the courage to throw away my passport. I figured a few months would be my limit, but I would try this seriously, as if it were to be my whole life. I felt uneasy, knowing I had an escape hatch—I could always call my parents, and they would send me money. But I wouldn't do that unless I were desperate.

I finally managed to sleep for a few hours, expecting to wake and realize that this plot was just a silly coke-dream. But when I woke, I still wanted to do it.

When I told Garry my plan, he was astounded and concerned but admiring. Of course, he also liked being the main beneficiary of my cash depletion. I was tempted to buy a carpet or a lovely *objet d'art* to send home, but acquisition seemed to contradict the spirit of becoming a sadhu. I gave more alms than usual to the beggars, but most of my money went to Garry and his friend Gilles for drugs. I went back to Hassan's twice to partake of cocaine with them, but these sessions never approached the clarity and camaraderie of that first high. However, I was perpetually high on the shock of what I was about to do.

Six days passed, and I still wanted to become a sadhu. I went to the railway station to reserve a seat on the train to Benares, but the trains were booked up for the next four days, and there was a long line at the booking window. The hell with it, I decided, I'll fly. I took a cab to the Air India office and booked a flight for the following morning. Then I went back to the hostel, sorted my possessions, and made up the two small bundles I would carry. Garry came to say good-bye. I gave him my notebook of journal writings and short stories.

"Here, I'm not taking these. Read them, okay? And then do whatever you want with them.

Throw them out or use them for toilet paper, I don't care."

This bravado was false. The external evidence of my creative spirit, raw though it was, never ceased to amaze and delight me. Those writings were hard to part with. But a sadhu could not carry such trappings of ego.

"Listen," Garry said. "If you get tired of being a sadhu, write to me in Goa, and I'll send you money to come meet me there." He wrote down his address and then gave me a long hug. "I hope you'll be okay."

"I will. I'm not sure what I'm doing, but I know I can do it."

"Good luck. And be careful."

"Thanks, and I will."

He left. I never heard from him again.

2 PRACTICE

After the week-long high of anticipation and vertigo, the first day in Benares was like a punch in the belly. Between my past and the future I had constructed in my imagination, there was a gap called the present that had to be bridged. Although I had ideas on how to proceed, the necessary resources were not laid in my lap, and I floundered; meanwhile, all these people were watching me.

I had my head shaved in a barber shop, fending off the barber's groping hands, and then took my first bath in the Ganges. I had expected a spiritual orgasm to afflict me at the sight of Mother Ganga, but I saw only a river, not as wide as the Hudson where it reaches Manhattan. Soon the sun had dried my skin and the shawl I had bathed in. I changed into my white *kurtha* and *longhi* and sat on the stone steps of the *ghat* while I pondered my next move.

I still had about fifty rupees and didn't know what to do with it. I would feel guilty asking for alms or shelter if I had so much money. Should I spend it? Give it away? Keep it for a hotel in case I couldn't find a place to sleep? No, that was cheating. So I had to get rid of my money and find out where the sadhus slept and ate. I should ask a sadhu, logically, but so far I hadn't seen any among the crowds of pilgrims plunging into the river and milling on the *ghats*. I had to be in the wrong part of town.

I walked along the river to the funeral pyres. Again, disappointment: I couldn't get close enough to see the gory details of burning bodies, nor did I detect the reputedly horrid stench of burning flesh.

I headed back up the twisting streets and stopped at a corner to buy *pooris* and chickpeas. There stood a man dressed in burlap, barefoot. He looked like a sadhu, although his rags were not orange. I gave him a coin and some of my food and tried to explain to him what I was seeking, but I barely knew any Hindi. He led me around to several temples, up and down the *ghats*, shooing off other beggars who tried to approach me. He pointed out items for me to buy: carrots, incense, a small religious book I couldn't read. I followed him passively, miserable because I didn't know what to do while I waited for him to show me the freebies. I couldn't tell whether he had understood anything I had said.

People stared. A hairless, light-skinned young woman dressed in the white clothing of a pious Hindu man, following a scruffy beggar with dirty burlap tied to his body. Occasionally people tried to warn me away from him. Their concern was touching, but I didn't want anyone telling me what to do. It made me angry because it made me doubt myself. I kept reminding myself that others' opinions didn't matter.

We went into a restaurant. I ordered potato curry and *chapati*. He didn't start eating until I was finished and didn't sit with me. I wondered if he considered me too impure to eat with him, since I was a foreigner and not a Hindu. I paid for the food, avoiding the entrepreneur's eyes, and we left.

We went to another temple. He had me throw down a few coins and imitate him in a brief ceremony, bowing and muttering before the altar. I tried to pay attention, since he might be showing me something important.

I was finally roused into action when he hailed a rickshaw to take me to a hotel. Sadhus simply did not sleep in hotels. Or was he hoping to sleep with me?

AFTERNOON OF A SADHU

Someone had told me of an American woman who had been a sadhu for many years and was still living in Assi, a district at the southern edge of the city. When I told my escort I was going to see a friend, he pleaded for a rupee, which I gave him. I told the rickshaw driver to take me to Assi Sangam and settled back in relief.

I didn't know how much to pay for the ten-minute ride to Assi. Rather than worry about overpaying, I gave the driver a ten-rupee note and walked away. That got rid of some money. I felt almost poor enough to beg. After I went to a store and bought a small metal food bucket with handle and lid, I had ten rupees left—just over a dollar. I decided it was all right to tuck it away in case of emergency.

Next I looked for Sita, the American sadhu. She was said to live near the riverbank. I walked two blocks, past white-washed house fronts, children playing in the dirt, women filling buckets from a tap in the street. At the end of the street was a large muddy area scored with streamlets and gullies. To the right, green fields; straight ahead, the broad river; to the left, a ghat. I skirted the mud and the flower sellers' stalls with their heaps of saffron marigolds. Buffalo stood in the shallows while laughing young men scrubbed their flanks. Shacks stood in the muddy area, lines outside them hung with saffron clothes. Could they be people's homes? Sadhus' homes? Sita's? I didn't have the courage to go up and knock on the doors. My relief at having taken some action began to trickle away.

I walked along the ghat until I saw a white building with towers that resembled a temple. I climbed the steps to a courtyard. A chubby man wearing a white *longhi* and plaid blanket sat at an altar in a small chamber, decorating the Shiva *lingam* with flowers and red powder. He smiled at me and invited me, in Hindi, to sit down.

"Sadhu?" he asked. I was elated. Someone had recognized my costume. I asked if he knew of a place I could sleep. He indicated that I should wait. He finished with the altar, locked the doors, and went into the main building. I stared out across the river, trying to focus on my breathing and forget my terror. After about twenty minutes, a lean, middle-aged man rode up on a bicycle with a briefcase dangling from the handlebars. The man in the plaid blanket came out and said a few words to him, pointing at me.

"You are coming from which country?" the man asked.

"America."

"Why you have this, the hair cut off?"

"I like it that way."

"And why you are dress in this man's clothes all white? You are sadhu?"

"Yes."

"Ah-hanh." He nodded, looking perplexed.

"Do you know someplace I could stay for the night?"

"Yes, perhaps."

"I don't have any money."

"Of course." He frowned. "Why find you yourself in this situation?"

I dropped the corner of my shawl, which I had been twisting and folding. "I'm trying to learn about myself."

"Ah-hanh." He sighed. "Well, I can give you a room, but for this night only. Tomorrow you must find another place. Of course, if you have no other place, I will not turn you away, but this hostel is for old people who come to Benares to die. You should not stay here."

He brought me to a small, cold chamber with a concrete floor and a door onto an alleyway. The room was completely bare.

"Is this room adequate? It is perhaps not enough comfortable for you."

"No, no, it's fine, it's very good."

He left me to arrange my blankets and shawls on the floor. I was steeling myself for the cold night, when there was a knock at the door.

A teenaged girl came in. She asked me my name.

"I gave up my name when I became a sadhu. I am waiting for a guru to give me a new name."

"But what is your name?"

"I have no name."

"But you must have a name."

"No."

"Then what shall I call you?"

"Whatever you like. Why don't you give me a name?" She wasn't qualified to give me a real spiritual name, but she was so perturbed by my anonymity, I had to think of a compromise.

"I will call you Shubha," she said.

"What does that mean?"

"It means 'beauty'." Later her father lent me a Hindi-English dictionary which translated *shubha* as "accuracy, straightness". I wish I could remember her name.

She left, returning soon with a plate of fried sweets and a thick quilt that kept me warm through the night.

Sitting on a rooftop, bathing in the afternoon sun, stoned on good hashish, I listen to the drone and twang of the sitar. It traces patterns of sensation on the layers of my mind, the interlocking tones and rhythms manipulating fibers of feeling, alternating red/gold or thrilling terror/courage.

Fernando has been playing sitar for six years. He practices six hours a day. He shows me the bandage on his finger. "It hurts. If I stopped playing for a few days, it would get better. But how can I not play?" He is a tall, gentle Spaniard in his thirties, with a brown ponytail. His guru gives him a music lesson twice a week. Fernando will have to leave India in three months, when his visa runs out, but he doesn't want to leave his guru.

He is giving pointers to Martine, a beautiful French gamine, who has just started playing sitar. She has $300 left, and no prospects for income. She is also worried she has lice.

AFTERNOON OF A SADHU

I told them what it was like being a sadhu. "Maybe I should do like you when my money finish," Martine said. "Is interesting but very scared." She gave me a five-rupee note, which touched me. Fernando invited me to visit his rooftop again.

It was almost dusk, and I decided to try reversing my Circadian rhythm. If I could sleep in the sun in the daytime, I could spend the nights walking and meditating and wouldn't have to worry about keeping warm or finding a room. In this way, I would also meditate more, without the distraction of daytime crowds, thus justifying my existence as a sadhu.

So I set off for a walk along the river. Assi was on the very edge of the city, which turned abruptly into vast fields of marigolds and orange asters, cultivated for their holy color to sell as devotional offerings at the hundreds of temples in Benares. I followed paths into the fields and stood giggling in the midst of acres of saffron dots. Finally I reached a long foot-bridge that crossed the river to a village. I had considered fasting, but it seemed better to take one thing at a time. I spent two rupees on a *poori* and some spiced vegetables in a leaf cup. As darkness fell, gas lanterns were lit with a hiss, and the stalls of vendors became white-yellow islands in the dark. I turned down a side street and heard steady music and chanting. On the porch of a small temple sat a man with a drum and two men with small cymbals. All three were chanting,

> *Hare Krishna Hare Krishna*
> *Krishna Krishna Hare Hare*
> *Hare Rama Hare Rama*
> *Rama Rama Hare Hare*

Every few minutes the drummer would change the rhythm, and the others would follow. They nodded and smiled as I sat down and joined the chanting. Twenty minutes later they smiled at me again as they stood up and departed, leaving me alone.

I set off down the road again. It was turning colder as I left the village behind, and the road became a highway. I wandered down a misty, moonlit path past a farmhouse and into the fields. The quiet was broken by occasional trucks on the highway, the distant barking of dogs, a rustling breeze in the branches. My sandaled feet moved through damp grass, and I was chilled.

As I walked, I tried to make sense of my being here. An adventure, mad but brave. A test of my fortitude and resourcefulness. A step into the unknown. I recalled an incident from my last night in Bombay. I had had dinner in the hostel dining hall, but I hadn't been able to eat the pot roast, so I offered it to other people at my table. They all refused, and I ended up going from table to table, not wanting to waste the pot roast but feeling silly walking around the room with a plate of meat. No one wanted it. Finally the Indian waiter took it and muttered, "You stop that now. Go sit down," as if to a child or a mental patient. His attitude made me wonder if I were not going slightly crazy. Now I decided it was all right to be crazy. Or was it? I argued with myself:

"You don't belong here. You're making a fool of yourself."

'I don't care. I'm here to learn something in my own way. I don't care what people think."

"But it's ridiculous to be freezing in a field in the middle of the night, broke and alone *by choice*. No sane person would do that."

"It doesn't matter. I don't have to go by other people's standards. Just shut up!"

I sat down in the dirt path, where there was no dew, and tried to meditate, but the battle of thoughts disrupted my concentration. Just as my body was beginning to relax and warm up, I heard voices and footsteps. Two men appeared, looked at me in surprise, and began to question me in Hindi.

AFTERNOON OF A SADHU

"*Sadhana*," I said, putting my palms together as if praying. "Sadhu," pointing to myself.

They muttered and gesticulated. Nervously, I asked, "Benares?" One of them pointed toward the road, and I walked away quickly.

My memories of the rest of that night are vague. I recall a wild-looking man who led me to a tiny shelter and built a fire. I had to snarl to keep him from touching me, and I left when the fire died away. There was a farmhouse where dogs barked and a family slept outside. Two boys offered me a bed, and I ran. Near a pump station at the edge of an irrigation ditch, I found a small rope bed, where I lay for a while but couldn't relax, hearing the approach of real or imagined footsteps.

Exhausted, I climbed a grassy bank and reached the highway again. I had given up the idea of meditating. Twice more I stopped and managed to sleep fitfully in the cold: once, wedged in various odd positions among the trunks of a huge tree; once, on a wooden platform in front of a closed truck stop. I walked for hours, stilling the raging doubts with fantasies of becoming a Himalayan hermit and returning home an inscrutable sage. I crossed an interminable bridge, high over the Ganges. To the south, a few amber lights marked Benares. I had no idea what time it was. I wished the night would end.

When I finally reached the end of the bridge, there was a small railway station and a road sign that read "Benares 1 km". I passed a night watchman who stared at me in astonishment. Alongside the station was a concrete platform with a roof. The floor was covered with people—beggars, I suspected—of all ages, huddled under blankets. Many of them were coughing, and the sound was repulsive. But maybe I could sleep here. I found a spot and lay down with my shawl and blanket, but the floor was very cold, there wasn't enough space to stretch out my legs, and the coughing was unbearable. I felt sorry for the people who slept there every night. I just couldn't do it.

I went back out and past the watchman. He stopped me and asked in English, "From where?"

"America."

"Alone?"

"Yes."

"Boy or girl?"

"Girl."

"*Girl?*" He nodded thoughtfully. I felt uneasy and started to edge away. He put his arms out towards me, spreading them in a hugging gesture, and asked, "Yes?"

"No!" I barked. "Sadhu!" And I fled up the road.

It was another long walk into the center of town, past the shuttered stores. Tea stalls were open here and there for the drivers of infrequent trucks. Twice I approached stalls where lean men gazed at me in the white light of the sizzling lanterns and asked, "How much?" Firmly, I ordered tea. The sweetness and warmth gave me a push onward.

I reached the center of town as darkness was fading. Under an arcade lining a row of shuttered shops, ten stray cows were settled. Among their steaming bodies, it was warm. I wondered why the beggars didn't sleep here. Just then a grey cow lurched to her feet and let loose a copious stream of urine, answering my question. I found a concrete block attached to the building where I could sit without getting soiled and fell asleep surrounded by the cows, while Benares woke up.

Martine lived in a rented room at the end of an elbowed alley, part of the maze of little streets just off Assi Sangam. There were several empty rooms in the building, and the landlord lived elsewhere, so Martine suggested that I sleep in one of the tiny, bare rooms. For several nights, I arranged all my belongings carefully beneath and around me and slept. I awoke twice each night and uncurled my cold-stiffened body from the concrete floor to walk to the toilet down the hall. These accommodations were satisfyingly ascetic.

I continued to see a lot of Martine and Fernando, whose moral support kept me from going under. Their admiration was vital because it proved I was an intrepid adventuress, not a self-deluded fool. I avoided going to the rooftop at mealtimes because I knew they didn't have much money.

Other Westerners fed me occasionally, but I wanted a more reliable and traditional way of getting food. Fernando had mentioned an Italian sitar student who had once been a sadhu and now lived in a house by the river. I sought him out and asked how he had eaten in his begging days. His answer was vague, but he mentioned a temple where the poor were fed twice a day. That evening I took a walk and found a large temple surrounded by a metal fence. The gates were closed, and there was no food line. Maybe it was the wrong temple or the wrong time of day, although 6:00 p.m. seemed like dinnertime. Why hadn't I gotten more details from the Italian? Why couldn't I find a soup kitchen, of which there must be scores in Benares? Why didn't I have the fortitude to fast? I finally used up three rupees of my stash in a restaurant and felt better.

Next I tried begging. It seemed like an important part of the sadhu experience, not only because I needed money to eat, but also because it would teach me humility. On my way to a famous Durga temple across the river, I had a conversation with four young men. As I was leaving, I dared myself to ask them for *paise*, and they refused. They laughed and said they were poor. I walked away, hurt more by the laughter than the refusal.

I was famished that night when I returned to Assi with only 10 *paise* -- a penny -- in my pocket. I could buy a snack of two *samose* at a stall on the street for 35 *paise*. In desperation, I stopped a young man and asked for 15 *paise*. He stared at me in surprise and asked why I needed the money. I told him I was a sadhu and needed to eat. He stood there for a moment, deciding whether to believe me. Finally he shrugged, gave me a coin, and walked on. I felt tense and shrunken, like an insect some kind soul had decided not to step on. I never begged on the street again.

Then I had my encounter with Chai Baba. After ten days in Benares, I felt like just another traveler from the West, sitting around with my friends all day and smoking hash. Except that I was sponging off people instead of paying my way. Fernando had recommended that if I needed any help I should go to Chai Baba, who ran a tea shop in the center of Assi and knew all the Westerners in the district. I didn't know what to ask him for, but out of curiosity, I went to the shop.

I ordered tea, prepared by the Baba himself, who turned out to be young and handsome, not the grizzled sage I had expected. Short and stocky, with shoulder-length black hair and deep bronze skin, he looked around quietly, as from within a dusky room. He frightened me a little.

After serving my tea, Chai Baba sat down and stared at me. "You are in trouble."

"No, I'm not in trouble."

"You look in trouble. Why you are dressed in this and shave the head? You are sadhu?"

"Yes."

"And why?"

I told him about getting stoned with Garry in Bombay and deciding to live on the edge.

"Junkie is bad people. You should stay away."

I saw red but said nothing.

"You are hungry?" I nodded. "Sit over there and I will give you food."

He brought me eggplant curry and *chapati* from the stove, and I ate gratefully while he served other customers.

"I have plan for you," he said. "Come."

Leaving the tea shop in the charge of a friend, he led me across the street and down an alley. He unlocked a blue wooden door and lit the gas lamp. We entered a small room with a luxuriant carpet and pillows on the floor. Lines of light showed at the edges of the shuttered window.

"You live here with me. I teach you yoga. Every day we meditate and do asana. You leave this sadhu. It is not for you."

I was confused. I wanted a teacher, but I was determined to remain a sadhu. Finally, I asked, "I would have to make love with you?"

"Yes, of course."

"No, I'm not interested."

I stomped out, seething. What did he want, a white mistress to show off to his friends and to follow him around? I wasn't that abject, at least not yet. But his criticism had shaken me. I went to the *ghat* to bathe and then lay in the sun watching the other bathers: women struggling out of their saris beneath gold and fuchsia wrapcloths; men pounding soapy clothes on the steps at the edge of the water. I washed my *kurtha* and *longhi* and spread them out to dry. I tried to enjoy the sun, but I was too upset. I was tempted to call my parents and ask them to send money, but I couldn't give up after only a week and half. And I hadn't even tried the walking-in-the-country bit yet. I wasn't quite ready for that but I had to get out of Benares.

Bodhgaya, where the Buddha attained enlightenment, was only a few hours away by train. I really ought to make a pilgrimage to this sacred place. And it was a small town; maybe it wouldn't swallow me up as Benares had.

I bundled up my possessions, said goodbye to Martine and Fernando, and walked to the railway station. I slept inside on the floor among the other beggars and travelers and caught an early morning train. The ride was short, and no conductor passed by to ask for my nonexistent ticket.

In Bodhgaya, I ran into Christine, a Swiss girl I had met on a meditation retreat in Sri Lanka. She was impressed by my sadhuhood and decided

AFTERNOON OF A SADHU

I was a worthy cause. She rented us a double room at the Burmese *vihara* and took me to the Tibetan cafés to eat. Every evening we went to the Zen temple for meditation.

We visited two monks, Bhante Akasa and Bhante Kassapa, our meditation teachers who had come to India on pilgrimage. Bhante Akasa, a Jew from New York, didn't act surprised when I told him what I was doing. I was disappointed. "You'll probably learn something," he said.

Christine and I went to a Japan Buddha Sangha temple in nearby Rajgiri and chanted "*Namyo-ho-renge-kyo*" for three hours in exchange for a night's lodging. We visited the sect's shining white "Peace Stupa", a temple on a hill, near a ruin where the Buddha himself had lived and taught. Sitting on the ancient stone foundation, I wondered what the hills had looked like when the Buddha had gazed on them. I thought about my meditations in the Zen temple. At least I was practicing, but it didn't make me feel any different. My life in Bodhgaya was too domestic, being supported by a friend. If I was really on a spiritual path, I had to take the plunge and put myself in the hands of the universe—in the hands of the Indian people. I had failed as a street beggar, but in the countryside I would be forced to beg, completely at the mercy of people's generosity. By trusting in them to take care of me, I would begin to chip away at my ego. But I had to relinquish all security.

The only security I did have was the strength of tradition. I wanted to make sure I was recognized as a sadhu, so the next day I went to the market in Gaya and bought a lump of ochre dye. I washed my white clothes in it, according to Akasa's instructions, and they turned a muddy orange. "So you're really going to do it," he said. "Good luck."

At the end of the week, I left on foot.

3 THE REAL THING

I am standing in the middle of a field. All I can see are green wheat and blue sky. The wheat, waist-high, sways in the sun. What am I doing, alone in this great gorgeous field? I don't belong here. I certainly wouldn't be here if I hadn't given away all my money and dyed my clothes. Who else would be so stupid? No, who else would be so brave!

Drunk on green and feeling special, I set off again through the wheat. I come to a patch of plants that reach up to my head, and the path disappears. I push through where the plants are thinnest, trying not to crush them. I think

Benares is straight ahead, about 80 miles.

An hour later, I'm resting under a tree on a roadside. People pass by, pausing in confusion to stare, then shrug and go on. After a while, a crowd of three has gathered, a boy, a young man, and a woman. I look up, and the man speaks in English:

"You are coming from?"

"Bodhgaya."

"Your country?"

"America."

A lot of nodding and murmuring.

"Going to?"

"Benares."

"By walking?"

"Yes."

"Why you do not take train?"

"I like to walk. I have no money."

Great confusion. An American without money? Embarrassed, I turn away, wishing they would go.

"Excuse me, please. You are sadhu?"

"Yes."

"Who is your guru?"

"My guru's name is Bhante Akasa. He lives in Sri Lanka."

"Who do you worship?"

"I worship *Buddha-Bhagwan*."

I am shaky about this answer. Is it acceptable to take advantage of the Hindu institution by invoking my Buddhist background? The people seem impressed, but I'm still uncomfortable. I am professing religion for the sake of the lifestyle, rather than vice versa.

"Excuse me, please. You are male or female?"

"Female."

"Yes, thank you."

"I must go now. Goodbye."

Laughing to myself at their gaping faces, I pick up my bundles and walk on.

VIOLET SNOW

My first village, sleepy and peaceful in the romantic evening light. Two cows wander past, but there are no people. I walk down the street of a ghost town. Finally I turn a corner and see a man sitting on a porch. I convey to him in my limited Hindi that I am seeking nourishment and shelter for the night. Flustered, he takes me to a group of women, who stand by the street and stare at me. I cannot make my request boldly or gracefully. The women complain that they are poor. By now a dozen of them are standing around me, exasperated by my inability to understand their questions. They are suspicious but curious. They point to my bundles, which I empty onto the ground, eager to prove that I am living in poverty. I worry my toothbrush and plastic soap dish look like luxuries, and I'm glad to have left my D.H. Lawrence novel back in Bodhgaya. They give me water and two thin rice cookies and order me to leave. I am hurt, panicky, near tears. Where will I sleep?

AFTERNOON OF A SADHU

Across the main road is another village. Because I am desperate, I force myself to go in. Immediately I meet three men. This time I am more crafty and ask only for a place to sleep. The men lead me to the covered porch of a house. The ends of the porch are enclosed on three sides and strewn with straw. At one end stands a buffalo, in the middle a wooden bed. At the other end, a blanket is laid on the straw for me. I collapse onto the stale straw, which will infest my clothes and blankets with bedbugs.

In a few minutes, a crowd has formed. The conversation by the roadside is repeated, this time in Hindi, with many gaps and much repetition, as I struggle with the language. These people are perplexed but patient, smiling indulgently when I don't understand. I sit on display, stimulated by the attention, trying to pretend I am not paranoid and terrified that I will do something wrong.

Someone asks me if I prefer rice or *chapati*. I'm relieved I don't have to ask for food. It arrives an hour later, delicious rice and vegetables. I am shifted to the bed. As I am getting sleepy, musical instruments are brought. In the harsh light of gas lanterns, the crowd settles down to hours of singing and drumming, through which I sleep fitfully. When I awake in the morning, there are fifteen people asleep in the straw. Some of them have bad coughs. They are all sleeping in thin shawls. One man gets up and unwraps his son from a piece of cloth which he then ties around his own waist to cover his bare legs. I have been sleeping under two shawls and a blanket. People begin to mill around, ignoring me. A woman milks the buffalo and gathers up its steaming chunks of dung.

The woman sends me around the corner of the house with a brass vessel of water for my morning ablutions. No one has asked me if I want a bath. It's rather cold, but isn't a sadhu expected to bathe every morning?

AFTERNOON OF A SADHU

This morning is sharp and misty, delicately shaded in pale blues and grays. Behind the house are more houses, stolid whitish rectangular buildings with thatched roofs. I squat to urinate in the cold grass. When I look up, there are women hovering outside the neighboring houses, hiding behind the corners of their saris. I look back to see men peeping around the corner of the house. This is embarrassing. How am I going to change my underwear? I'll have to stop in a field along the road.

I wash my face without looking up, brush my teeth, and return to the porch. Am I expected to do *asanas* or prayers? Maybe meditation will suffice. I sit in half-lotus on the bed and try to focus on my breath. But people still want to talk to me. An old man arrives, and the others crowd up to listen. He conducts the standard conversation and tries to convince me to take the train to Benares. I decide it's time to leave. But I have a guilty conscience. After a lengthy inner debate, I offer them my blanket. They refuse, saying that I need it and that they have no way of splitting it amongst them. If I were deeply concerned, wouldn't I just run off, leaving it there? But I really want to keep the blanket, so I pack it into my bag, relieved.

Then the old man hands me a rupee. I'm astonished. Another man gives me a rupee, a boy gives 35 *paise*. A more well-dressed fellow presses eight rupees on me for a train ticket. With tears pouring down my face, I walk off in the yellowing morning light.

I followed the road until it veered south. Benares was to the northwest, so I set out across the fields until I came to a muddy river. I walked downstream to a wide, shallow section, hitched up my *longhi*, piled my bundles on top of my head, and slogged to the opposite bank. There I sat in the grass to let my muddy feet dry. I could see huts and haystacks nearby. Lunch time, I thought.

AFTERNOON OF A SADHU

I was about to head for the village when four men appeared. They dropped onto the grass and began asking me questions in Hindi. Their jesting tones made me apprehensive. After a few routine questions, one of the men asked if I were carrying a gun. He said he was a policeman and wanted to search my bundles. He reached over. I stood up, trying to act indignant instead of scared, and made for the village. I heard the men laughing, but they didn't follow me.

I slipped in the ruts between the pale houses. I asked a young woman for a drink of water, and she sent a boy inside for a glass and a *lota*. As I drank, a crowd gathered. I answered questions haltingly, doing my best to appear hungry, because I was afraid to ask directly for food. Finally I heard the word "eat". But I wasn't sure if they were saying "Have you eaten?", to which I should answer "no", or "Do you want to eat?", to which I should say "yes". There were several minutes of confusion. I was embarrassed and frustrated, and the villagers must have thought me demented. At last I recognized the word for "stomach" and remembered the phrase "*Pet khali hai*"-- "Stomach is empty." We were all relieved.

A boy poured water over my hands, and a woman brought a huge plate of rice with a tiny clump of highly spiced peas and potatoes. Vegetables, I thought, must be in short supply. I ate slowly as the people watched, whispering. Disturbed by their poverty, I offered a rupee as payment, but they refused it. When I headed out across the fields again, a contingent of boys followed me, the oldest pleading with me to go back to Gaya and take the train to Benares. It was dangerous in Bihar state, he said. *Dacoits* would rob and kill me. Turning back felt like a violation of my principles. I had resolved not to fear anything and believed that showing anger would protect me. So far, it had, but the men at the river had unnerved me, and I had heard of bandits in

Bihar, one of the poorest parts of India. The boys were persistent. I tramped back across the fields and caught a bus on the road to Gaya. At five o'clock the next morning, I was again asleep on the floor of the Benares railway station.

I consulted a map and found that the railroad went in a straight line from Benares to Allahabad, the next major city on the Ganga. I figured I couldn't get lost. I got on a northbound train, got out at a country stop, and walked to the end of the platform, where I found a path. And so for the next week, I plodded along beside the railroad tracks.

I was happy with nothing to do but walk in the sun and watch the landscape, no immediate concerns except where to eat and sleep. I would stop at a village and ask for water, and the surprised people would offer me food, or, at night, a bed to sleep in. On the few occasions when they didn't offer, I had to dredge up the nerve to ask directly. These people, either too suspicious or too poor to provide for me, always directed me to someone who could. My Hindi had improved, and communication became enjoyable, although repetitive. My arrival in the village always drew a small crowd. I liked the attention, which made me feel important, and most people treated me with warmth, which made me feel accepted. Now I was truly a sadhu.

As I left my path to enter a village and seek a night's shelter, I would walk in the softness of evening light and long shadows, observing the sweetness of men returning from the fields and the day's work over. The ambiance of family, boys playing in the spaces between houses (not quite streets), girls helping their mothers cook dinner. The sunlight gold-green over the fields of cane or mustard or young wheat.

In one village I was taken on a tour of the sugar cane operations. A teenaged boy led me around with a group of children and showed me where the sheaves of cane brought in from the fields were cut into shorter lengths. The cane was crushed in a machine to extract its juice. The boys gave me a cup of foaming juice. They taught me how to crack and peel a stick of cane with my teeth so I could chew on the juicy stalk. We returned to the house to wait for dinner, and they laughed at me as I practiced gnawing on chunks of cane. The older boys peeled pieces for the small ones to chew. After dinner, I fell asleep promptly and slept soundly.

In the morning, the women said I should stay for a while, but I insisted on getting back on the road. Halfway to the railroad tracks, I looked around at the opulent fields and thought, why not —such a peaceful place; it might be nice to stay for a few days. I ran back to the village and said I had changed my mind. People stared at me in consternation, and I realized that their invitation had been only politeness. Embarrassed, I went back to my long walk.

I knew the country people were poor, but they didn't seem so. I loved the primitive living conditions: mud-and-dung floors, a field in place of toilets, water drawn from a well, sticks cut from *neem* trees instead of toothpaste and toothbrush. To work hard in the fields around the rough houses, and then to rest with one's family, sharing a simple life governed by the seasons, the cycle, the flow of nature: the people looked serene. Or was this just romance? I knew there were famines and droughts and taxes. I didn't know what working for hours each day in the field was really like. I was not the one drawing water from the well and lugging it home. I was barely scratching the surface of their lives, and they would show a guest their best face.

After a while, I began to feel guilty. Despite their poverty, these people were so generous. In their minds, it was good karma to give, especially to a sadhu; but they were performing a duty. Maybe they didn't really want to feed me. And

AFTERNOON OF A SADHU

who was I, rich by their standards, to take food from their mouths? True, I had no money, but simply by going to the city and making a phone call, I could transform myself into an affluent American.

Oh well, it's in the tradition; the sadhu has the right to except alms in exchange for her renunciation. It's part of a purification, a dedication of oneself to God. I was not begging out of laziness, I was attempting to transform myself. But was I getting any closer to God? I wasn't even doing a regular spiritual practice: little meditation, no *asanas*. What was I doing to justify taking food from poor people? Was I doing any good to the universe, besides providing entertainment?

Thinking along these lines led me into despair. If only I had a teacher, or a real sadhu to guide me. I wasn't even sure what a sadhu was supposed to do. Maybe the villagers thought I was bogus because I didn't do *asanas* or didn't clean myself properly. I cringed, wondering. So God provided me with a sadhu.

Terrain along the tracks turned rough, and I wandered off onto another path and got lost. I was in a land of scrub, mild slopes, and irregular fields. The path wound in arcs and forked, and I had no idea which way was north because the sky was overcast. I tried to convince myself that having no direction didn't matter in this occupation, but I soon became thoroughly depressed. I lay down in the stubby grass and tried to sleep, but it was midafternoon. I got up and dragged myself onward. I came across some boys and ask them how to get to the Ganga. They waved vaguely and looked at me like I was crazy. Then I stumbled upon a railroad track. But I wasn't sure which way to go. It seemed I should still be east of the railroad line but what if this were only a branch line? I didn't want to end up back in Benares.

AFTERNOON OF A SADHU

After trudging for another hour, I reached a train station. Bigger than the usual country stop, it had four tracks and two roofed platforms. A few people were sitting on the platforms. I was tired, so I joined them.

I looked around, intending to ask someone which way was north, and there he was—a sadhu, in his late twenties, ruggedly built, with long hair and heavy eyebrows. He was sitting on a blanket next to several small bundles. I went over and asked him which way was Allahabad. He pointed, and then looked at me more closely.

"Sadhu?"

"Yes," I answered, in Hindi.

"You are a woman?"

"Yes."

"Where are you going?"

"To Allahabad."

"Alone?"

"Yes."

"I am going to my guru. Will you come with me?"

"All right."

Wow. A real sadhu, with saffron clothes, bare feet, beads and strings around his neck, his long hair twisted up funny on his head. And he was taking me to meet his guru. Talk about dreams come true. I plunked my possessions down next to his.

A train pulled in, and we climbed into a boxcar. Grimy men were sitting on the floor. My new friend perched on a high crate, and I stood near the open doors, watching the passing fields of pea plants and flowering mustard. I was impatient to get to my education, but he didn't speak English, and my Hindi was too limited for the kind of conversation I wanted to have. Once he mumbled something about *asanas*, indicating that we'd have to do them later, since we couldn't practice on the train. An encouraging morsel. So I had to wait.

We got off at a small station to wait for a connecting train. The sadhu disappeared for a few minutes and came back with a snack, two *samose* for each of us. By now the sun had set, and it was getting cool. He spread out his blankets in a corner of the platform, which was deserted, except for an occasional beggar or passerby. I wrapped myself in my shawls. He lay down between his blankets and motioned for me to do the same. I felt nervous, but I was getting tired, so I finally lay down at the very edge.

He touched me, hesitantly at first, and then suddenly he was on top of me, with all my wrappings, including my *longhi*, up around my waist, and then he was inside me for a few hectic, rabbity strokes, and I was praying no one would notice us in the dark. The whole thing took maybe three minutes, and then we were lying separate between the blankets again, and I was pulling my clothing back into place, confused. I hadn't expected that. How naïve of me. I thought sadhus were supposed to be celibate. Was this one corrupt? Or perhaps he was a *tantric* yogi. But tantric sex was supposed to be a ritualized, slow and ecstatic coupling, not a sordid quickie for one person. The act had been repulsive. On the other hand, I hadn't had to put up with it for long. I wanted something from him, so I decided to wait and see.

The train pulled in, and we found an empty compartment. He immediately pressed me down on the wooden bench, raised my leg, and as we cleared away the layers of material, entered me from an unexpected angle. But someone was coming, so this session only lasted two minutes. Disgusted but still hopeful, I propped myself in a corner and fell asleep.

In the morning, we disembarked at a small town. As he led me up the dusty street, the sadhu looked happy—I assumed because he was about to see his beloved guru. Turning off the main street, we came to a brick archway with a wooden gate. We entered a walled yard with gardens on the sides and a long, low house facing the gate. A middle-aged woman was drawing water from a pump. She greeted the sadhu and then called out to the house. A tall man emerged. He looked to be in his fifties, with a straight back, long grey hair, and a scraggly beard. To my disappointment, he didn't look particularly wise. The two men embraced, both of them talking very fast. I was introduced briefly, and the guru nodded, staring. He pointed out a spot on the verandah where I could rest, and the woman brought me water to wash with. The men went into the house.

I waited a long time for something to happen. The woman brought food, and I ate. I walked around the yard, looking at the pink and red flowers and baby vegetables. I sat in the sun and made several efforts to meditate. Occasionally the guru would come out and peer at me from the other end of the porch, and then go back inside without speaking. The woman washed clothes in the yard, weeded the garden. Her malevolent glares began to unsettle me. Was she jealous? I wasn't dressed immodestly, but I was young and white and therefore exotic. The more I thought about it, the more I began to suspect that I had not been brought here for religious instruction. The idea of being used as a concubine by two corrupt men humiliated and incensed me. I gathered up my bundles and informed the woman that I was going to Allahabad. She grinned. The men came out of the house, looking surprised. I stayed just long enough to ask how to get to the railway station, and then I was back on the road.

My next sadhu spoke English. The sun was close to setting when a character in orange pulled his bicycle up beside me and invited me for dinner. He pointed to a turn-off not far up the road, where a dirt track crossed the fields to a cluster of buildings. Then he pedaled on, elbows, knees, and robes all flapping.

This yogi was middle-aged, plump, and talkative. The buildings and surrounding fields were his ashram, and he had a few disciples, including a hawk-faced, wild-haired man dressed in white. This fellow and two younger men joined us for dinner on the porch. The sadhu spoke to me in English and to them in Hindi, and I was ill at ease. He encouraged me to stay for a few days, and I said I might.

I was given a bed in the women's quarters. I fell asleep instantly but was soon awakened by a hissing sound. The room had two doors, one into the hallway and the other to the outside. The latter one consisted of two hinged pieces of crude wood, like shutters, with metal rings on the inside. The rings were tied together with a piece of rope that kept the doors shut. Through the crack between the doors, a man was calling to me, asking me to let him in. I sat up, frightened. The rope didn't look secure, and he was reaching his fingers through the gap between the doors. Finally, I called out, "No! Go away!"

The women woke up and began to shout from the next room, trying to chase the man away. Now that they were awake, he had nothing to lose and came through the hall door into my room. It was the hawk-faced man. He touched my arm, and I shrank away, yelling. The women crowded into the room, cackling and flapping their arms, and drove him out. They continued to cackle indignantly, commiserating with me. I thanked them and burrowed back into my blankets.

After breakfast, I announced my intention to leave. The women nodded approvingly, but the yogi was chagrined. "Why do you wish to leave already? You must come at least to see our temple. It is just that way, across the field." The women murmured, but he silenced them. Uneasily, I agreed to look at the temple, and we set out with two of the young men. Halfway there, the hawk-faced man joined us, and I had sudden visions of a gang bang. I turned around and said I was leaving. When they protested, I broke into a run. As I passed the buildings, the women waved to me. In the hot sun, I took the road back to the railroad tracks and continued north.

I passed through an assortment of villages. In one, a family offered me a meal, but I wasn't hungry; I only wanted water. They sat me down behind their house, where an ox plodded in a circle at the end of a wooden shaft. The shaft was connected to a cane-juice squeezer, from which the husband gave me a glass of juice. He also presented me with lumps of *gur*, the brown sugar they made from the juice. The couple seemed so pleased to have something to give. For several days, I nibbled on the *gur* when I was hungry between villages. It was a bit of security.

One afternoon, the railroad tracks suddenly veered to the right, deviating from the straight line I had relied on all week. Then there was a river, with a bridge, high over the water, leading into Allahabad. It took me half an hour to get across the bridge. The sun was bright, the steel girders were swollen with heat, the river was olive-green and restless. I was excited at the prospect of a new city. Once the novelty of the villages had worn off, I had begun to suffer from a sense of aimlessness, and I welcomed the change of scene. But where would I stay? How would I eat? I knew nothing about Allahabad. But being on a bridge is like being on a train: there's nothing to do but wait until you arrive.

On the other side, I found a small white temple and a plump man in saffron. I lingered around the temple, hoping for some clue to food and shelter, but I was too timid to ask questions. At an intersection, a big man with a briefcase was trying to hail a rickshaw. I asked him which way was the center of town.

"Where do you wish to go?" he inquired.

"I'm looking for a place where I can stay for free. I have no money."

AFTERNOON OF A SADHU

He didn't show surprise. "I am going to visit my sister and brother-in-law. They are staying in a *dharamsala*, a hostel for pilgrims. You might be allowed to sleep there are a few nights without paying. It is a very safe place, with respectable people. I will introduce you to my sister's family."

The rickshaw dropped us in front of an old brick building. We walked through an archway into a large courtyard. Someone said I could sleep in a wooden bed beneath a balcony, and the gentleman's relatives offered to feed me. They cooked their meals on the balcony outside their room.

The next day I bathed for the first time in a week, in the broad plain of water where the Jumna River flows into the Ganga. Farther up the bank, on the ghat, I could see the colored plumage of pilgrims, whose baths were rituals filled with devotion. They honored the gods, and they honored the two rivers that met here. I wondered what devotion felt like. I felt lonely and sad.

On the way back to the *dharamsala*, I stopped to look at a group of laborers who lounged on the sidewalk, waiting for work. They probably had approximately the same amount of money in their pockets as I did. And they were standing on the street in Allahabad, just yards from where I stood, but all their lives they would be laborers, and they would never travel past the borders of India, and they would never have much more money in their pockets than they did right now. While I, in a matter of weeks, could be a million miles away, teaching English or working in an office and making more money in a year than one of them would make in his whole life. It didn't seem fair. I stared at them for a long time across this vertiginous gulf and groped for some kinship. House, family, friends -- I had none here. Love, desire, pain, anger -- too general; I had to speak to them to find out what they loved and hated, and even were there no language barrier, I would not have known how to approach them. A man squatting against the wall flicked a fly from his cheek and scratched his head. He already looked tired. Perplexed, I went back to the *dharamsala*, where my new acquaintances served me lunch.

The people here were kind, but I kept meeting the pious, not the mystical. I wanted to be around yogis, and I knew I could find them in Rishikesh. I was tired of walking, so I took the train. I had heard that sadhus are sometimes allowed to ride trains for free. Anyway, ticket checking by Indian conductors was sporadic. I hadn't encountered any conductors on my rides between Benares and Bodhgaya. And if I did get thrown off the train, I would just go back to begging in the villages. The train pulled in to Haridwar in the early afternoon. I went down to the *ghats*, which were covered with black and white tiles in checkerboard patterns, and wandered through the crowd.

Hawkers of flowers for altars: the faithful need marigolds. Men who rent out little platforms with umbrellas to protect from the sun while the bathing faithful change their clothes. Prayer booklets and incense and *samose* and *pakore* and little metal vessels and badly printed pictures of Shiva, Shakti, Krishna, Parvati, little blue boys and multi-limbed men. Beggars, with and without limbs, and the fat Brahmin priests and fat pious women with jewels. I scowled at them. I wanted my holy cities holy. This was a carnival.

At the end of the checkered *ghat*, on a long grassy strip, a group of sadhus were cooking a meal. One of them, a tall, gawky Indian, called out to me in English.

"I met you in Goa. Do you remember?"

"No, not really."

"Yes, on the beach, in my house. My name is Ganesh. You are American, yes?"

I had met a sadhu named Ganesh, but I remembered him as a small man. But then, I had only seen him lying down, from the door of his hut, where I sat with his American girlfriend, Nora. They teased each other and joked about sex. I liked them. She was brassy and ironic, and he had the presence of a tiger cub. This was undoubtedly the same man, but now he reminded me of Ichabod Crane.

"Oh yes, I think I remember."

"So you are sadhu now."

"Yes. I just walked from Benares to Allahabad and stayed in the villages."

"Sit down and eat with us. Then you can tell me what happened."

I shared their meal, peeking apprehensively at the fierce-looking sadhus, who ignored me. I washed my plate in the river – swift-running here in the Himalayan foothills – and then sat with Ganesh in the grass. I started to tell him about Bombay and Benares, but he interrupted me. Instead of commenting on my adventures, he babbled some story I couldn't follow about another American girl who put him up at a hotel in Calcutta.

"There was even hot water in the shower! Oh, you should have seen it, it was amazing!" I said nothing. "Look, I have an idea," he went on. "I go today to an ashram in Rishikesh, where the swami is my very good friend. I still have some money Nora gave to me. I buy food for us, and we stay some time in this ashram. Then we go in the mountains and practice sadhana. I can teach you *asanas* and meditation. Okay?"

Marvelous, a direction and a teacher. Just what I needed. But could I trust this guy? Not that he would harm me, but he was irritating and goofy. Maybe he wasn't a real sadhu but merely a lazy man who leeches off foreign women. On the other hand, he was offering to support me, not take money from me. And Nora obviously liked him. Maybe I could trust her judgment.

I said yes.

AFTERNOON OF A SADHU

He took me to Haridwar's main drag. In a tea shop he made a casual inquiry, sent me outside, and then emerged with a ball of paper. Inside it was a brown, sticky lump of opium the size of a ping-pong ball. He explained that he was an addict and had to eat a little of it each day to keep from getting sick.

We took a horse-drawn *tonga* cart upriver to Rishikesh, a ten-minute ride, and climbed a hill above the town. It was dusk when we reached the walled compound of the ashram. The swami was glad to see Ganesh, but all the rented rooms were occupied. He said we could sleep on the roof for free.

We joined six Westerners who were gathered around a fire, passing a *chillum* of hash. The star of this group was a quiet Austrian who had pitched his sleeping bag on the porch of the little Shiva temple. A chatty British couple and their female friend occupied two of the rented rooms. Another was taken by two Dutchmen who were almost out of money and casting around for drug deals. We sat through several passes of the *chillum*, Ganesh talking as freely to the Westerners as to the swami, who hovered intermittently behind us. I spoke little, smiled at the blond Austrian, who smiled back.

Finally Ganesh and I retired to the roof and spread out all the blankets we owned. The night was already cold, and the roof was open to the wind. Ganesh said we'd better share our body warmth, or we'd freeze. I disliked this idea, but I dreaded the cold. Once under the blankets, I could not refuse to let him make love to me. But I did so through clenched teeth and detested both of us for it.

I wonder if he thought I enjoyed the sex. In a perverse way, on the physical level, I did, and that in itself was degrading. I felt guilty for my mental resistance. He had been kind to me so far, and he was providing for me. Who was I to judge him as inferior to me, or unworthy of my sexual favors? But I didn't like him. I watched my mind wrestling with alienation and distaste, trying to be open to another human being and his needs. Humiliation built up as I raged at finding myself obligated to do something I didn't want to do. I found at tang of pleasure in the punishment of his fingers squeezing my breasts too hard, hurting them. I dug my nails into him, a touch of my pain going outward. He fussed over his sagging erection and finally stopped to do some deep breathing, asking for patience. At last he was hard enough to enter me and said proudly, "My *tantra* always works." At some point my jaw unclenched from exhaustion, and I gave up the mental fight. That didn't stop me from hating him in the morning, and fearing that I was behaving like a prostitute. But I seemed incapable of doing otherwise.

    I kept myself remote from Ganesh, speaking to him as monosyllabically as possible. He seemed unfazed by my coldness. We mingled and smoked with the Europeans. I would cringe as he cheerfully suggested a *chillum* of their hashish, apparently oblivious to the glances they would exchange. I would throw in a few glances of my own, to dissociate myself from Ganesh, but I was, after all, sleeping with him.

I didn't know what to do with myself. I wandered around the compound or the streets, sinking into depression. Once I went to the tea shop just outside the ashram and tried to make conversation with the Westerners there but failed. When I wandered back into the ashram, I discovered that my change purse was missing. It had contained all the money, I owned, nine rupees —just over a dollar. I searched the ground and the tea shop but didn't find it, so I assumed it was stolen. Despondent, I roamed the compound, still combing the ground and muttering angrily. I told Ganesh, who told the swami, who seemed amused by my agitation. Here I was, a sadhu, cultivating poverty and non-attachment, in an outrage over nine rupees. My self-loathing deepened.

The next day I couldn't move. I lay between the blankets, mentally reviling myself and Ganesh for the previous night's sex. He went out and got us tea and *pooris* for breakfast, prodded me out of bed to eat. I was going numb. He announced that we would wash our clothes.

I followed him to the river, where smooth stones led to the water's edge and rose up out of the shallows. The sky was a mild blue, and the mountains were close at hand. Ganesh patiently sorted through my things and helped me wash them, beat the soapy clothes on the rocks when I lost interest, rinsed them and showed me where to spread them out. I pretended I was a puppet, relieved to be incapable of judgment or will. I sat quietly in the sun waiting for my clothes to dry. Ganesh told me when to turn them over so they would dry on the other side. He decided when they were dry enough to fold, and then led me back to the ashram. I sat on the roof, huddled in a blanket, while he went out. He brought okra, potatoes, and spices from the market and took me into the yard to show me how to cook. I watched, still comfortably paralyzed, and then ate in silence. Ganesh made no attempt to draw me out of my catatonia. In the evening we smoked with the Europeans, and I smiled hopelessly at the Austrian.

Sex reawakened my revulsion for Ganesh. In the morning I announced my plan. Garry had told me to write to him in Goa if I wanted to quit being a sadhu, and he would send me money to join him. From there I could go back to Tehran and make enough money teaching English to return to India. I wrote Garry a letter and rushed to the post office. It was Thursday. If he got the letter on Saturday and sent the money out right away, I might have it by Monday. Nothing happens that fast in India, but I was desperate to believe it would. On that hope I could survive the next few days.

AFTERNOON OF A SADHU

Ganesh was running out of money. Sometimes he stood on line at a temple to get us free food. I ate, smoked, and hoped my way through four days. I took Ganesh into town to a pharmacist and made him buy me birth control pills. I had left mine behind in Bombay, thinking I would be celibate as a sadhu.

Finally, Monday. I rushed down to the post office. No letter. Back into despair.

Tuesday. No letter. I couldn't take any more. Maybe Garry was in Bombay or in jail. I could be waiting forever. So I implemented my contingency plan.

I packed up my things, and Ganesh offered to escort me to Haridwar. He asked for my address in the United States because he expected to go there and wanted to visit me. Mortified, I made up an address in Rochester, where I'd never been. I've always felt a little guilty, wondering if he tried to find me in Rochester.

VIOLET SNOW

The train to Delhi left late in the evening and was packed. In the vestibule at the end of each car, men sat on their luggage. I wedged my two bundles into a little space by a window, sat down on them, and fell asleep curled up against the wall. The implacable rattling and swaying of trains always made me feel cradled and safe — especially now that I had escaped Ganesh and Rishikesh.

In the middle of the night, a conductor woke me and asked for my ticket.

"I don't have one."

"You must buy."

"I have no money."

"Why not?"

"I am a sadhu."

He squinted at me, as if trying to decide whether I were pulling his leg. I pointed to my shaved head and opened my shawl to show him my orange clothes. He shrugged and walked on. The men around me laughed softly, and I went back to sleep.

AFTERNOON OF A SADHU

It was early morning, hazy and powder blue, when I stepped out of the New Delhi train station. The mobs of porters and hawkers were beginning to arrive. I walked to Jan Path, a street in the city center, and reached the post office just as it was opening. I found the telephones and placed a call to my parents. They were glad to hear from me. They had been apprehensive about what I had described in my last letter as "a walking tour of the Ganges." They agreed to send me $500. Ganesh had given me a few rupees, and I bought some rolls for breakfast and then took a bus to Mehrauli, where I knew of a hostel that cost two rupees a night.

I was no longer a sadhu.

EPILOGUE

The question continued to haunt me: had I done something courageous and spiritual, or egotistical and absurd? Certainly I had failed as a sadhu—I had given up after only six weeks, I had acquired no spiritual discipline, and I had not found a teacher. But six weeks is a long time for a girl from Poughkeepsie to live without material possessions. If I could achieve this feat, then what could I not do?

My goal was not really to be a sadhu for the rest of my life, but to learn, to discover resources hidden inside me. I found that I had courage, that I had the sense to extricate myself from the sticky situations I blundered into, and that I was better off on my own than when I followed someone else around. I also discovered the disturbing truth that one cannot remain aloof from the negative judgments of some people while seeking reassurance in the approval of others.

Above all, I acquired the confidence to follow evidently absurd paths without regrets. I set a pattern for the rest of my life, which has been rife with intriguing absurdities ever since.

Years later, I came to see this adventure as an initiation process, a testing and tempering of my essence. Lacking a sense of wholeness, I threw off the shaky scaffolding of my identity and went into emptiness and danger to construct a new self.

In tribal cultures, initiations are carefully orchestrated by the community's elders. This supervision does not mean that the process is without risk. West African elder Malidoma Somé writes of initiates who have died on the journey through other realms. For the majority who survive the ordeal, the community witnesses their success and celebrates their return to its collective, connective heart.

Like many youth who embark on modern-day initiatory ordeals—often by way of drugs, crime, cults, illness, or madness—I returned from my journey without witnesses. I managed to find my way into community, but I did not readily tell my story. As Malidoma remarks, the initiate needs people to witness and acknowledge her experience, in order to give it meaning. Otherwise, the ordeal is likely to be repeated in other forms, until a meaning is found.

I thank you for being my witness.

GLOSSARY OF HINDI WORDS

Apke liye, babaji. - For you, old man.
asanas - yoga postures
Buddha-Bhagwan – Lord Buddha
chai - spiced tea cooked with milk and sugar
chandu - liquified opium
chapati - unleavened bread
chillum - cone-shaped pipe
dacoit - bandit
dharamsala - rest house, hostel
ghat - flight of steps leading down to a river
gur - brown sugar
kurtha - loose shirt worn by men
lingam – pillar symbolizing the God Shiva
longhi - cloth wrapped around the waist and legs
lota - water vessel

neem - tree with aromatic, medicinal bark
paise – coins, one *paisa* being worth 1/100 of a rupee
pakore - fried snacks (plural of *pakora*)
poori - puffy, fried bread
sadahana – spiritual practice
samose - potato-stuffed savory pastries (plural of *samosa*)
tantric – referring to *tantra,* a set of mystical practices that incorporate a science of sex
vihara - monastery

ABOUT THE AUTHOR

Violet Snow is a freelance journalist who lives in the Catskill Mountains of upstate New York. She has been an herbalist, a computer programmer, an actress, a poet, a photographer. She is writing a book about her ancestors and African spirituality. She plays in the band Foamola with her husband, Sparrow; her daughter, Sylvia; and composer Lawrence Fishberg.

Made in the USA
Charleston, SC
01 June 2013